The 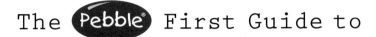 First Guide to

Nocturnal Animals

by **Joanne Mattern**
Consulting Editor: Gail Saunders-Smith, PhD

Consultant:
Deborah Nuzzolo, Manager
SeaWorld/Busch Gardens
Education & Conservation Department
San Diego, California

Mankato, Minnesota

Pebble Books are published by Capstone Press,
151 Good Counsel Drive, P.O. Box 669, Mankato, Minnesota 56002.
www.capstonepress.com

 Books published by Capstone Press are manufactured with paper
containing at least 10 percent post-consumer waste.

Library of Congress Cataloging-in-Publication Data
Mattern, Joanne, 1963–
    The Pebble first guide to nocturnal animals / by Joanne Mattern.
    p. cm. — (Pebble books. Pebble first guides)
    Summary: "A basic field guide format introduces 13 nocturnal animals.
Includes color photographs and range maps" — Provided by publisher.
    Includes bibliographical references and index.
    ISBN: 978-1-4296-3307-9 (library binding)
    ISBN: 978-1-4296-3860-9 (paperback)
    1. Nocturnal animals — Juvenile literature. I. Title. II. Series.
QL755.5.M38 2010
591.5′18 — dc22   2009004927

About Nocturnal Animals

Animals that are active at night are called nocturnal animals.
They come in many shapes and sizes. The animals featured in
this book are some of the common nocturnal animals. The lengths
given in this book include measurements from head to tail.

Note to Parents and Teachers

The Pebble First Guides set supports science standards related to
life science. This book describes and illustrates 13 nocturnal animals.
This book introduces early readers to subject-specific vocabulary
words, which are defined in the Glossary section. Early readers may
need assistance to read some words and to use the Table of Contents,
Glossary, Read More, Internet Sites, and Index sections of the book.

Table of Contents

Bat 4

Crocodile 6

Eel 8

Firefly 10

Frog 12

Gila Monster 14

Lemur 16

Moth 18

Opossum 20

Owl 22

Raccoon 24

Skunk 26

Tiger 28

Glossary 30

Read More 31

Internet Sites 31

Index 32

Bat

musky fruit bat

Wingspan: 6 inches to 6 feet
(15 centimeters to 1.8 meters)

Weight: .5 ounces to 3.3 pounds
(14 grams to 1.5 kilograms)

Eats: insects, mice, fruit

Lives: forests, prairies, deserts, towns

Facts:
- only flying mammal
- some live 30 years in the wild

Bat Range

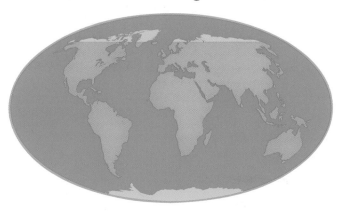

☐ worldwide, except polar regions

Natterer's bat

Crocodile

Nile crocodile

Length:	4 to 23 feet (1.2 to 7 meters)
Weight:	up to 2,000 pounds (900 kilograms)
Eats:	fish, snakes, turtles, crabs, birds
Lives:	swamps, marshes
Facts:	• swallows stones to help digest food • snout is long and narrow

6

Crocodile Range

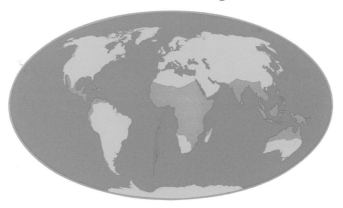

☐ North America, Central America,
South America, Africa, Southeast Asia, Australia

American crocodile

Eel

American eel

Length: .3 to 13 feet (.1 to 4 meters)

Weight: up to 144 pounds (65 kilograms)

Eats: insects, crabs, fish

Lives: rivers, bays, seas, oceans

Facts:
- is a fish that looks like a snake
- female freshwater eels return to ocean to lay eggs

Eel Range

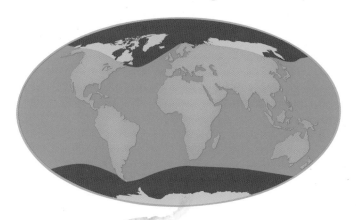

□ □ worldwide, except far north and far south

moray eel

Firefly

Length: less than 1 inch (2.5 centimeters)

Weight: less than 1 ounce (28 grams)

Eats: insects, snails, worms

Lives: forests, near streams and ponds

Facts: • some glow in the dark to find a mate
         • also called lightning bug

Firefly Range

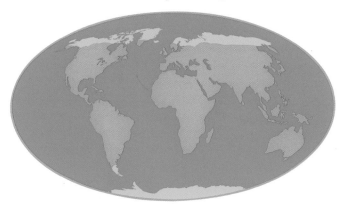

□ worldwide, except polar regions and southern tip of South America

Frog

red-legged frog

Length: .5 to 12 inches (1 to 30 centimeters)

Weight: up to 6 pounds (up to 2.7 kilograms)

Eats: insects, snails

Lives: rain forests; in or near rivers, ponds, lakes

Facts:
- young are called tadpoles
- males with vocal sacs have a loud call

Frog Range

worldwide, except polar areas and oceans

tadpole

painted reed frog

vocal sac

13

Gila Monster

Say It: HEE-lah MON-stur

Length: 18 to 24 inches (46 to 61 centimeters)

Weight: 1.5 to 3 pounds (.7 to 1.4 kilograms)

Eats: rats, birds, mice, frogs, eggs

Lives: deserts

Facts:
- bite contains venom
- lives in underground burrows

14

Gila Monster Range

☐ southwestern United States and Mexico

red ruffed lemur

grey mouse lemur

Length: .5 to 2.8 feet (.2 to .9 meter)

Weight: 1 ounce to 15 pounds
(28 grams to 6.8 kilograms)

Eats: fruit, flowers, insects

Lives: rain forests

Facts:
- many live in trees
- excellent sense of smell

Lemur Range

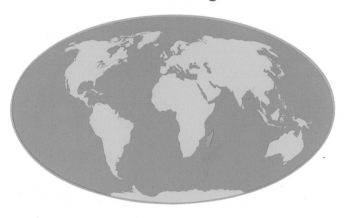

☐ Madagascar

ring-tailed lemur

Moth

promethea moth

Wingspan:	less than 1 inch up to 12 inches (2.5 to 30 centimeters)
Weight:	less than 1 ounce (28 grams)
Eats:	nectar, fruit, tree sap
Lives:	woodlands, rain forests, towns
Facts:	• have been found in Arctic • use antennas to smell

18

Moth Range

☐ worldwide, except Antarctica

discolored renia moth

Opossum

Say It: uh-POSS-uhm

Length:	2.5 feet (.76 meter)
Weight:	9 to 13 pounds (4 to 6 kilograms)
Eats:	insects, snails, mice, fruit, grass
Lives:	grasslands, forests
Facts:	• acts dead when scared • uses its tail like a long finger

Opossum Range

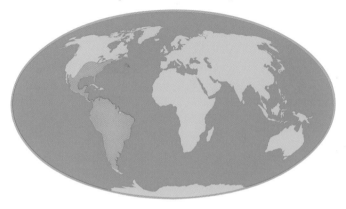

☐ North America, Central America, South America

female with young

elf owl

Wingspan: 6 inches to 5 feet
(15 centimeters to 1.5 meters)

Weight: 1.5 ounces to 10 pounds
(42.5 grams to 4.5 kilograms)

Eats: mice, insects, birds, frogs

Lives: forests, woodlands

Facts:
22
- turns head almost completely around
- the elf owl is the smallest owl

Owl Range

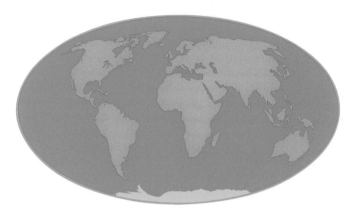

⬜ worldwide, except Antarctica

screech owl

great horned owl

Raccoon

Length: 2 to 3 feet (.6 to .9 meter)

Weight: 4 to 23 pounds (1.8 to 10.4 kilograms)

Eats: frogs, mice, fruit, fish, garbage

Lives: forests, fields, towns

Facts: • fur on face looks like a mask
         • uses its toes to hold things

Raccoon Range

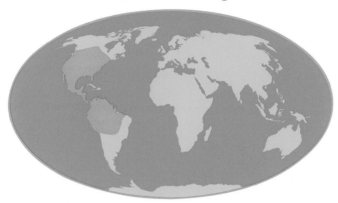

☐ North America, Central America, South America

young

Skunk

Length:	1 to 2.8 feet (.3 to .9 meter)
Weight:	7 ounces to 14 pounds (198 grams to 6.3 kilograms)
Eats:	insects, mice, eggs, plants
Lives:	woodlands, prairies, deserts, towns
Facts:	• lives in small groups • sprays a smelly liquid when scared

Skunk Range

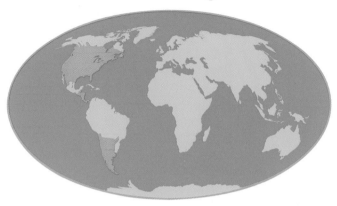

☐ North America, Central America, South America

young

Tiger

Bengal tiger

Length: 7 to 11 feet (2 to 3.4 meters)

Weight: 165 to 675 pounds (75 to 306 kilograms)

Eats: antelope, monkeys, deer

Lives: forests, swamps

Facts:
- each has a different stripe pattern
- endangered; only 5,000 to 7,000 left

Tiger Range

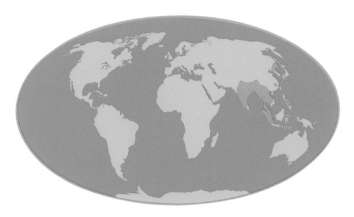

southern and eastern Asia

Siberian tiger

Glossary

antenna — a feeler on an insect's head

burrow — a tunnel or hole in the ground made or used by an animal

digest — to break down food to be used by the body

endangered — in danger of dying out

nectar — a sweet liquid found in many flowers

polar — having to do with the icy areas around the North and South Poles

sac — a part of an animal that is shaped like a pocket or bag

snout — the long front part of an animal's face, including the nose, mouth, and jaws

venom — a poison that some animals make

wingspan — the distance between the tips of a pair of wings when fully open

woodland — land that is covered by trees and shrubs

Read More

Clarke, Ginjer L. *Black Out!: Animals that Live in the Dark.* New York: Grosset & Dunlap, 2008.

Weber, Belinda. *The Best Book of Nighttime Animals.* Boston: Kingfisher, 2006.

Internet Sites

FactHound offers a safe, fun way to find Internet sites related to this book. All of the sites on FactHound have been researched by our staff.

Here's all you do:

Visit *www.facthound.com*

FactHound will fetch the best sites for you!

Index

burrows, 14

deserts, 4, 14, 26

eggs, 8, 14, 26

endangered, 28

forests, 4, 10, 20, 22
    24, 28

prairies, 4, 26

rain forests, 12, 16, 18

smell, 16, 18

swamps, 6, 28

towns, 4, 18, 24, 26

water, 8, 10, 12

woodlands, 18, 22, 26

young, 12

Grade: 1
Early-Intervention Level: 25

Editorial Credits

Katy Kudela, editor; Bobbi J. Wyss, book designer; Alison Thiele, set designer;
    Jo Miller, media researcher

Photo Credits

AP Images/John Harrell, 21; BigStockPhoto.com/M.P.T., 25 (right); BigStockPhoto.com/
TarasBoolba, 24; Brand X Pictures, cover (frog); Comstock Klips, cover (tiger); Corel, 20,
23 (both); Creatas, 29; Digital Stock, cover (bat); DigitalVision, 12, 28; Dwight R.
Kuhn, 10, 11; fotolia/EcoView, 13 (right); Getty Images Inc./National Geographic/
Tim Laman, 4; Getty Images Inc./Visuals Unlimited/Jack Milchanowski, 27 (right);
Getty Images Inc./Visuals Unlimited/Jim Merli, 14, 15; Getty Images Inc./Visuals
Unlimited/Steve Maslowski, 27 (left); iStockphoto/Liz Leyden, 6; James P. Rowan, 18,
19; Minden Pictures/Tom Vezo, 22; Peter Arnold/Biosphoto/Danna Patricia, 9; Peter
Arnold/WILDLIFE, 5; Seapics/Doug Perrine, 7; Shutterstock/David Thyberg, 16 (right);
Shutterstock/Eric Gevaert, 17; Shutterstock/Ferenc Cegledi, 16 (left); Shutterstock/
Holger Ehlers, 25 (left); Shutterstock/Ryan Morgan, 26; Shutterstock/Thomas Mounsey,
13 (left); Shutterstock/Tony Campbell, cover (owl); Visuals Unlimited/David Wrobel, 8